LEVEL 2

City and Country

Jody Jensen Shaffer

NATIONAL GEOGRAPHIC

Washington, D.C.

Table of Contents

CHAPTER 1

Places Around the World

Look out of your window!
If you live in a city, you will
probably see traffic, buildings
and lots of people.
A city is an urban area.

An urban area is a place where many people live and work. Every city is different.

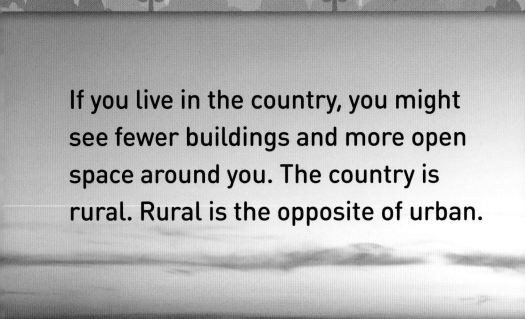

If you live in the country, you might see fewer buildings and more open space around you. The country is rural. Rural is the opposite of urban.

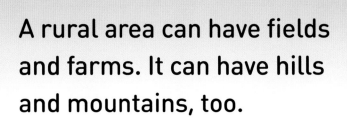

A rural area can have fields and farms. It can have hills and mountains, too.

YOUR TURN!

Look at the pictures.
Do they show a place that is urban or rural?

How do you know?

CHAPTER 2

City Home, Country Home

No matter where you live, there's no place like home. Many people in the world live in big cities. Cities are full of people.

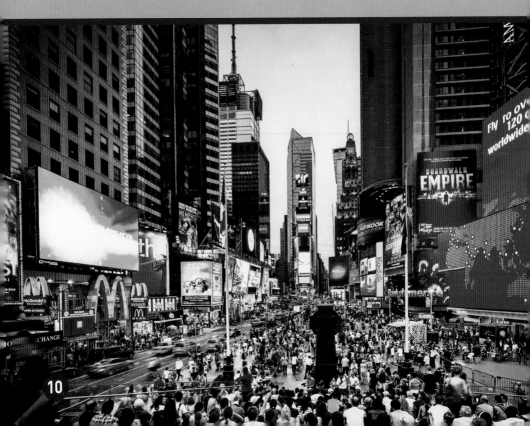

In big cities, homes are close together. Lots of people share the same outdoor space.

In the country, there is more space and fewer people.

There is space to run and play outside.

In some places, homes are a long way apart. In others, people must travel far between villages.

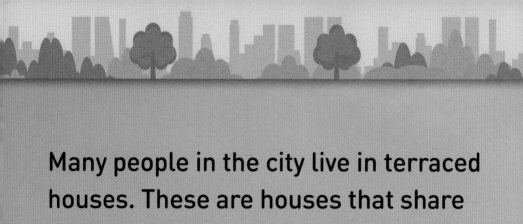

Many people in the city live in terraced houses. These are houses that share at least one wall with another home. Terraced houses sometimes look alike.

In the country, many homes don't touch each other. They don't always look alike.

In the city, people also live in blocks of flats. Tall blocks of flats have many levels inside. There are lots of homes on each level, and people can take the lift up and down.

In the country, most homes have fewer levels. Houses aren't as tall. They have more space to be wide.

City people don't always have much green space. Sometimes people make a garden in a shared space. They can grow vegetables and flowers in the shared garden.

In the country, many people have their own gardens. They can grow their own flowers and vegetables.

YOUR TURN!

Match the picture to the word.
Draw a line with your finger.

Word Bank

terraced houses

garden

flats

house

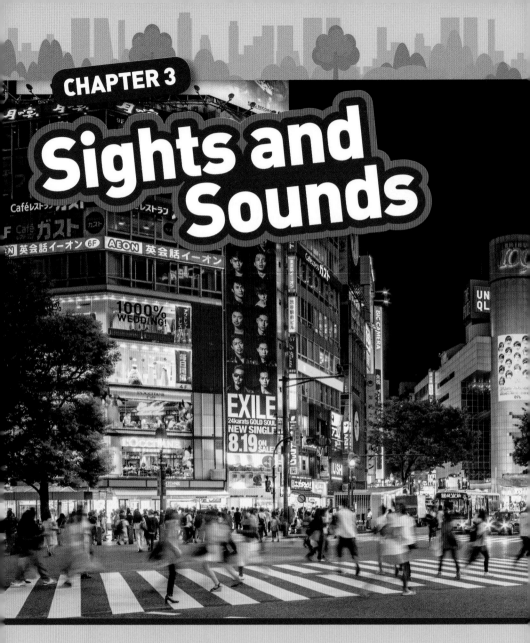

CHAPTER 3

Sights and Sounds

There are lots of things to see in the city. Tall buildings tower over people and traffic. There are bright lights and people all around.

You can see people
travelling in the city.
They take trains, buses
and taxis.

In the country, you might see rolling green fields full of cows or sheep. They eat the grass in the fields.

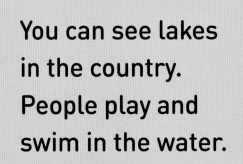

You can see lakes
in the country.
People play and
swim in the water.

Cities are full of sounds.
You can hear street musicians singing,
children playing in the park, and
friends laughing in crowded shops.

In the city, you can hear taxis honking and street sellers calling out loudly.

Sounds fill the country, too. You can hear cows mooing and trains whistling. Tractors rumble across fields, and insects chirp day and night.

In the country, you can hear water rushing in a stream. Frogs croak and fish splash.

There are lots of things to smell in the
city. People sell spicy food from street
stalls. The smell of freshly baked bread
fills the air outside a bakery.

You can smell many different things in busy cities.

In the country, you can smell freshly cut grass. The air is clean, and the smells of nature are all around.

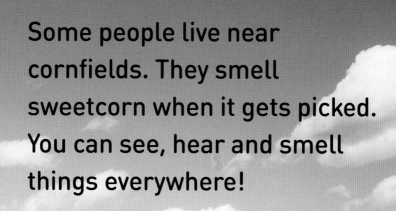

Some people live near cornfields. They smell sweetcorn when it gets picked. You can see, hear and smell things everywhere!

YOUR TURN!

Look at the pictures.
Tell a story about each one.

What would you see, hear and smell?

CHAPTER 4

Life in the City and the Country

No matter where they live, people in the city and in the country like to do many of the same things. They do sport. They ride bikes. They work and go to school.

Both city people and country people visit museums and go to concerts.

Some city people take walks for fun. People walk on trails that wind through city parks.

In the country, some
people walk in the woods.
They hike up and down
mountain trails.

Some city people take taxis and underground trains to get around. They might walk or bike to work and school. Sometimes people use buses to travel longer distances.

Some people who live in the country drive to work. Children sometimes go to school on a bus.

Students in city and country schools learn about the same things. Children everywhere study maths, science and history. They might take art and music classes, too.

Many students learn
about sports at school.
Children everywhere like
to run and play!

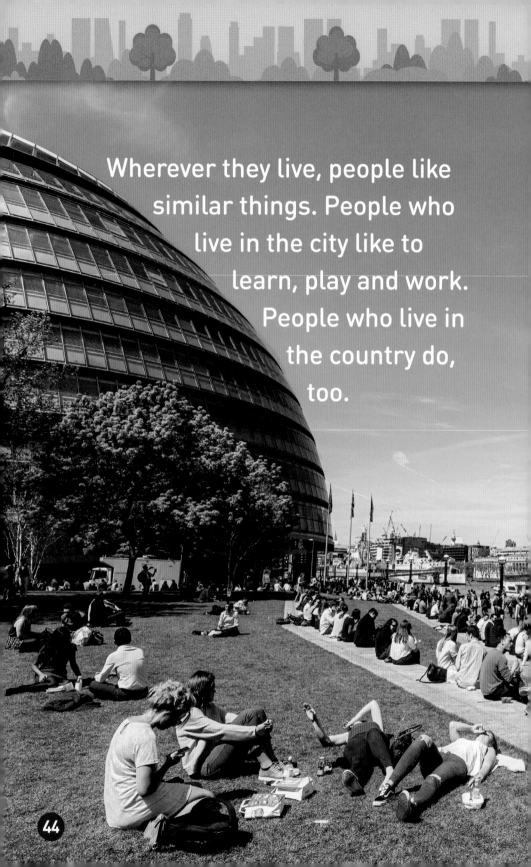

Wherever they live, people like similar things. People who live in the city like to learn, play and work. People who live in the country do, too.

Everyone likes to be with family and friends. No matter where home is, there is no place like it!

YOUR TURN!

What is it like where you live? What do you like to do?

Published by Collins
An imprint of HarperCollins*Publishers*
The News Building
1 London Bridge Street
London
SE1 9GF

Browse the complete Collins catalogue at
www.collins.co.uk

In association with National Geographic Partners, LLC

NATIONAL GEOGRAPHIC and the Yellow Border Design
are trademarks of the National Geographic Society, used
under license.

Second edition 2018
First published 2017

Printed and bound in China by RR Donnelley APS

If you would like to comment on any aspect of this book,
please contact us at the above address or online.
natgeokidsbooks.co.uk
cseducation@harpercollins.co.uk

Paper from responsible sources

Since 1888, the National Geographic Society has funded
more than 12,000 research, exploration, and preservation
projects around the world. The Society receives funds
from National Geographic Partners, LLC, funded in part
by your purchase. A portion of the proceeds from this
book supports this vital work. To learn more, visit
http://natgeo.com/info.

City
Cover: (UP) New York City; 1: Tokyo, Japan; 2: Hong
Kong; 4: Bangkok, Thailand; 5: (LE) New York City, (RT)
Cairo, Egypt; 10: New York City; 11: Guanajuato, Mexico;
14: Baltimore, Maryland, U.S.A.; 16: Bat Yam, Israel;
18: Brooklyn, New York; 22: Tokyo, Japan; 23: (INSET)
Rio de Janeiro, Brazil; 26: (UP) New York City; 27:
Calgary, Alberta, Canada; 30: (UP) Bangkok, Thailand;
(LO) Madrid, Spain; 31: Marrakech, Morocco; 36: (UP)
Mumbai, India; 37: (UP) New York City; 38: Kyoto,
Japan; 40: (LO) Chengdu, China; 44: London, U.K.

Country
Cover: (LO) Oregon, U.S.A.; 2: Switzerland; 6: (BACK)
Kansas, U.S.A.; (INSET) Indonesia; 7: (INSET)
Switzerland; 12: Norrbotten, Sweden; 15: (UP) El
Guayabal, Colombia; (LO) Underberg, KwaZulu-Natal,
South Africa; 17: California, U.S.A.; 19: Thailand; 24:
(BACK) Jackson Lake, Grand Teton National Park,
Wyoming, U.S.A., (INSET) Norfolk, England, U.K.; 28:
North Dakota, U.S.A.; 29: Japan; 32: Quebec, Canada;
36: (LO) Cape Town, South Africa; 37: (LO) Appleton,
Wisconsin, U.S.A.; 39: Beijing, China